Samuel Hall, 47 Years a Slave

Samuel Hall, 47 Years a Slave

HISTORIC PUBLISHING
©2017
(Edited Materials)

Samuel Hall, 47 Years a Slave;
A Brief Story of His Life Before and After Freedom Came to Him:
Samuel Hall b. 1818

Introduction
By
Orville Elder
b. 1866

LARGE PRINT EDITION

THE LIFE OF

Samuel Hall

WASHINGTON, IOWA

―――◯―――

A Slave For Forty-Seven Years

―――◯―――

BORN 1818

Samuel Hall, 47 Years a Slave

COPYRIGHTED 1912
BY
SAMUEL HALL
All rights reserved

JOURNAL PRINT, WASHINGTON, IOWA

SAMUEL HALL.

SAMUEL HALL

---o---

47 YEARS A SLAVE

---o---

A BRIEF STORY OF HIS
LIFE BEFORE AND
AFTER FREEDOM CAME
TO HIM.

Samuel Hall, 47 Years a Slave

COPYRIGHTED 1912
BY
SAMUEL HALL
All rights reserved

JOURNAL PRINT, WASHINGTON, IOWA

Samuel Hall, 47 Years a Slave

SAMUEL HALL
47 YEARS A SLAVE
A BRIEF STORY OF HIS LIFE BEFORE AND AFTER FREEDOM CAME TO HIM.

Samuel Hall, 47 Years a Slave

MARRIAGE OF A COLORED SOLDIER AT VICKSBURG BY CHAPLAIN WARREN OF THE FREEDMEN'S BUREAU.

Introduction

IT HAS been the good fortune of the writer of these lines to become rather intimately acquainted with Samuel Hall, colored, of Washington, Iowa. When I was in the grocery business Mr. Hall used to peddle vegetables and occasionally he would unload a few bunches of onions, radishes, early beets, new potatoes, tomatoes, celery, etc., at our store. On such occasions, it was always a pleasure to "jolly" the old man for he was old then--a dozen years ago. He was an old man thirty and even forty years ago, old as boys and girls look upon age, but always he has been young in spirit and even as a little child in his simple, Christian faith.

But, it was by means of those little business associations that I first got acquainted with Samuel Hall and later that acquaintance grew deeper and more cordial when Samuel Hall and John Wagner used to sit by the stove in the grocery on cold winter days and "argue religion." Those arguments used to grow quite animated at times, and Mr. Hall was frequently much put out because he had to stop and spit out a large quantity of Old Kentucky juice before he could safely give vocal expressions to his argumentative thoughts. He was always a ready arguer, however, and he and Mr. Wagner often made otherwise dull days quite endurable for those who were permitted to hear their controversies.

    Mr. Wagner, too, was a fine old character. He was a man who had come up from poverty into comparative wealth by means of indefatigable industry, sustained always by a goodly portion of that too rarely distributed but ever necessary element of success, common sense. He was a temperance crank. He loathed strong drink in every form and in that he and Mr. Hall were agreed, so it was frequently the case that this writer might by means of a little ingenuity becalm the threatening stormy climax of a religious controversy between these two men by gently leading their thoughts toward the evils of intemperance. That could generally be accomplished by mentioning that someone is "drunk again." Mr. Wagner died a few years ago. On his bed of sickness, however, and when he was at that threshold across which one-steps to be ushered into the greater eternity he did not forget his old colored friend, Sam Hall. He said to a mutual friend: "Tell Sam Hall that he is all right. Stand fast!"

And Sam Hall "still stands fast" and he believes that someday he will see John Wagner again for he knows that John Wagner's heart was right and when they do meet again Mr. Hall hopes that it will be in a place where the cuspidors will be so plentiful and so conveniently set about that he will at no time be interrupted in his arguments, for he has thought of a few "clinchers" that he wants to hand out to John Wagner when they meet again. And it will not be long, now, until Sam Hall will "pass across" too. He carries very nearly a century of years on his shoulders. He does not see so well as he used to see; he is not the physical terror that he was as a slave; he walks unsteadily with a cane and his days of hard work are past. But, his mind is alert and he entered into the plan of setting down in black and white a brief history of his life with youthful zeal. He fairly haunted the office of the writer, but was ever patient under trying interruptions and it has been a great pleasure to me to be helpful in arranging this story of Mr. Hall's life and in making an effort to express for Mr. Hall the great sense of gratitude which he feels toward the people of this community for helping to make his years of freedom such happy and fruitful years as they have been. He was a slave until he was forty-seven years of age, far past the half-way point in the average "old man's life, but he feels that God in his infinite wisdom and mercy has seen fit to bless him with a full, free life, even after a life of slavery.

ORVILLE ELDER.

Samuel Hall, 47 Years a Slave

BIRTH OF SAMUEL HALL.

THE STORY which we are presenting herewith is the story of the life of Samuel Hall, colored, of Washington, Iowa, and the story is one which illustrates in a most striking way the great injustice of slave life and it is but one of many thousands of like stories which might have been told by many colored people before they were gathered to that long home which we are taught to believe makes no distinction in color, or previous condition of servitude.

Mr. Hall is now, in the year 1912, in the 94th year of his age. He was born in slavery, in Iredell County, North Carolina, May 7th, 1818. He was the son of Samuel Hennick, who was born a free man in Liberia in the year 1756. The father at the age of 15 years was kidnaped, with his mother, and brought to this country, and both were sold as slaves into a family named Vanderver in Maryland. The mother would never work after she was sold into slavery, but pined away, never even learning the language of the people of this country. She looked always and waited in vain for the coming of her husband, her lover "Bingo" from the home land of Liberia.

Samuel Hennick, Mr. Hall's father, was first married in Maryland to a slave girl, who belonged to a neighbor of his master. Several children were born to this union, and then the father was sold away from his family, the mother retaining the children as the property of her master, and the father was taken into North Carolina. Here the father was married again, this time to Hannah Hall, who had been previously married also, and to the latter union Samuel Hall, the subject of this sketch, and one brother, Abe Hall, were born. While his father's Liberian name was Hennick, Mr. Hall took the name of his mother's master, "Hall," to whom he belonged by birth.

Samuel Hall has no way of knowing how many half-brothers and half-sisters he had. His father was married the second time at the age of sixty and Mr.

Samuel Hall, 47 Years a Slave

Hall was born some two years after that date. Mr. Hennick's children by his first wife were left in Maryland and Mr. Hall never got accurate information concerning them. Mr. Hall's mother had six children by her first husband and then the two, Samuel and Abe, by the second husband. The father died a slave in 1844 at the age of 88 years, in Iredell County, North Carolina. In this instance, too, the husband and wife belonged to different masters and Mrs. Hennick and her children were owned by Alex Hall, the family from which they acquired the name of Hall.

Samuel Hall, 47 Years a Slave

A PIECE OF PROPERTY.

WITH THE death of Alex Hall the more interesting part of Samuel Hall's life began. Alex Hall as the owner of Saml. Hall's slave mother and her children had kept them together, but with his death, in the distribution of his property, the slaves went as hay and corn and oats and pigs and cows go. In other words they were divided without regard to the wishes of the property. Samuel Hall's mother was inherited by Robert Hall, a strict churchman, a Seceder preacher, and he gave Mrs. Hall her freedom, taking his other slaves north with him and freeing them and there, still in the vicinity of Xenia, Ohio, the descendants of those freed slaves may be found. Mr. Hall's mother, however, did not go north even after she was freed. She chose to stay in North Carolina near her children.

Samuel was about twelve years of age when the separation of the ownership of his family, as above noted, occurred. He and his half-brother, Caesar, were inherited by Thomas Hall. Samuel Hall's full brother, Abe, was inherited by Hugh Hall, who also inherited Samuel Hall's half-brother, Isaac. Joseph Hall, the oldest of the sons of the father, Alex Hall, the original head of the family, inherited Samuel Hall's uncle, Peter Hall. Hugh Hall, owning Abe Hall, wanted Samuel Hall, the subject of this sketch, in order to keep the brothers together, so he traded Isaac Hall and wife to Tom Hall for Samuel Hall, and thus it was that Samuel Hall and Abe Hall, colored, full brothers, came into the family of Hugh Hall, white, as slaves.

 The life of Samuel Hall and his brother in the home of Hugh Hall was a happy life. Samuel was about 12 years of age when he became the property of Hugh Hall and he grew to manhood in this family and had the best of opportunities to educate himself and improve his intellectual condition. He took advantage of some of those opportunities and others he ignored against the advice of his master.

This master, Hugh Hall, was a humane man. He did not believe in slavery and he reared his Negroes as "free niggers." They were known far and wide for their high degree of intelligence and their capacity to do work and to do it intelligently, but the regular slave holders looked upon them as spoiled Negroes. Samuel and his brother, Abe, were never abused by Hugh Hall, nor would he allow others to abuse these slaves, or any other of his slaves. He was a champion of the black man's natural rights.

As an example of Hugh Hall's attitude toward the rights of the Negro Samuel Hall relates that in one instance Hugh Hall pursued a slave murderer to the gallows, it being a capital offense at that time for a master to kill one of his slaves.

This particular master had killed two of his slaves, one a girl slave and the other a boy. The circumstances in connection with the murder were terribly brutal. The master became angry with one of his girl slaves because she would not respond to his every immoral whim and he stripped her naked and tortured her by spearing her into efforts to climb a greased pole which he erected. When her hands slipped, in an effort to climb the pole, he would prod her with a sharp pointed piece of iron and in that way he tortured her to death.

A colored boy witnessed the killing and in the fear that the boy would tell, the master bound him and threw him into a brush heap which he set afire and the lad was cremated. The head did not burn, was discovered, and the circumstances already pointing toward the master as being guilty of murder, Hugh Hall pressed the case until the inhuman master was brought to the gallows and he confessed his crime before he was executed.

Situated in such a home as the Hugh Hall home it might appear that Samuel Hall's prospects were bright enough, even as a slave, but there were other conditions that conspired to eventually bring into Mr. Hall's life some of those heart-tearing tragedies which seem almost unbelievable in this day and age.

    Hugh Hall, like his brother the Rev. Robert Hall, did not believe in slavery and would have freed his slaves had he been free to do as he wished, but he was married to a woman who believed differently. She had been reared farther south and had quite different ideas from those that controlled her husband. She too had inherited slaves and a greater number than did her husband. When her husband suggested the freeing of his slaves she said that she would free hers too, and would also when that was done, return to her parents. Under that threat Hugh Hall kept his Negroes in so-called slavery but, as his wife said and as his neighbors knew, he spoiled them as slaves.

    Samuel Hall was with his master at the time of his death. They loved each other as brothers and when the master, Hall, died the grief of Samuel Hall was as genuine as would have been his grief over the demise of a dearly beloved brother. All the slaves of Hugh Hall respected and loved him and when he died they wept as if they had lost their best friend, and they had.

Samuel Hall, 47 Years a Slave

SOLD AWAY FROM HIS FAMILY.

WITH THE death of her husband Mrs. Hugh Hall immediately billed a sale of the grown slaves of the Hall estate. She claimed that she was afraid of these Negroes who had been reared by her husband as free Negroes and in this sale which she made was offered Samuel Hall, about whom we are writing, and who is today a resident of Washington, Iowa. He was sold on the block to a Mississippi-Tennessee plantation slave holder in the year 1855, then aged thirty-seven years. And there the real tragedy of Mr. Hall's life first came into evidence.

At the time of this sale he was a married man. Ten years before he had been married to Margaret Minerva Clark, a girl slave in the family of James Clark, who lived a few miles from the Hall plantation. This young colored woman had captivated young Hall and on the permission of their masters they became man and wife with no other formality, that being all that was required in that day and age.

Five children were born to this couple, Margaret, Ann, Augustus, Ellen and Adeline. The children were, of course, the property of the owner of the mother and it was from this family that Mr. Hall was to be sold. The day before the sale he helped to lift his old, insane mother into the wagon that carried her to the poor house. For years this old mother had stayed around where the children were, visiting from one to the other and serving as a sort of a granny doctor, but with this wholesale disruption of the family she became insane. She was sent to the poor house and Samuel Hall never saw her after that.

He kissed his wife and his children good-bye--four of the children, for the fifth, Adeline, was yet unborn--and went to the auction block and was sold off as we would sell a beef today. The wife and three of those children he never saw again. Two of the children, Augustus and Adeline, came north many years afterward when he sent for them. Adeline died a few months after arriving here, and Augustus is at present a prosperous citizen of the West Liberty, Iowa, community.

Samuel Hall, 47 Years a Slave

HE BRINGS $1,125.00.

SAMUEL HALL was a good piece of property. He was an intelligent Negro. But he was one of the so-called free Negroes and they were generally bought up by speculators who adopted taming methods peculiar to that day and age which very often accomplished the aim either by bringing the slave into subservience or killing him. All of the slaves offered by Mrs. Hugh Hall at her sale were sold to speculators excepting Samuel Hall. He was bought by a Tennessee man who wanted him for his own plantation, but with all that he had the reputation of being a bad man. Sam stood on a bench and was auctioned off for $1,125,00, $125.00 more than was brought by any of the other Negroes.

He did not see the purchaser, did not look to see. He was in a sullen mood, for the rearing he had received in the home of Hugh Hall had given him a proper conception of human rights. His soul rebelled against such subservience to men who called themselves masters and his temper was aroused to such a pitch that he was like a wild animal in a cage, conscious, in a way, of the hopelessness of his situation but none the less tamed, or willing to admit that he was justly restrained.

As he stepped down off the bench from which he had been sold, not knowing who had purchased him, the purchaser stepped up a little too close to Sam to suit him and he grabbed his owner and flung him back into the crowd.

Mr. Hall knows now that that was an unnecessary and an unwise thing to do, but he was not at that time in a tactful humor. He was in a mental frenzy, ready to fight to the death, to kill. He expected that they would attempt to shackle him then and there and he was determined in his heart that he would die before he would submit to such treatment.

The crowd evidently understood his mental attitude perfectly for pacific methods were adopted. A friend talked to him and told him that the purchaser was a good man. The purchaser trembling like a leaf came around and asked Sam if he would go with him.

"I'll go to hell with you if you want to go," was the answer the subject of this sketch gave to this new master.

After a while, however, he calmed down a little, agreed to go with his new master, went to his quarters and put on his good clothes and mingled with the crowd. He had sullenly refused to dress up prior to the sale. Coming forth in his good clothes, neatly attired and showing up his splendid physical manhood in better form Mr. Hall's new owner found that he had drawn a prize so far as appearances went any way.

They crowded around him asking "What will you take for the boy?" and the new master turned down an offer of $1,500.00 then and there.

HALF BROTHERS LOST.

AT THIS sale three half-brothers, a half-sister and other more distant relatives of Samuel Hall were sold to speculators. The half-brothers were named Peter, Ben and Caesar. Peter Hall was a well-educated Negro having taken advantage of the opportunities offered him in the Hugh Hall home and when he was put upon the block for sale he made a speech to the assembled crowd in which he protested against such treatment and against slavery. He was sold and immediately his hands and feet were shackled and Samuel Hall saw Peter for the last time as that unfortunate individual, dragging the heavy chains on his feet moved off toward the barn on the Hugh Hall plantation.

Mr. Hall never saw, nor heard from that brother again and has no knowledge of what became of him. He disappeared as completely from Samuel Hall's sight as he would had the earth opened and received his form into its cold embrace.

Samuel Hall, 47 Years a Slave

Ben Hall, too, was sold and never heard of or seen again by Samuel Hall and the half-sister, Zavorah, met with the same fate as did numerous of the other relatives. Caesar Hall was sold and bought right back into the same community and was well taken care of and lived a comparatively happy life. He died a few years ago. Samuel Hall learned of Caesar's fate after the sale through Augustus Hall, Samuel's son, who came north when Mr. Hall sent for him.

Sam might possibly have escaped from slavery had he chosen to make the effort. In the Hugh Hall home, however, the real evils of slavery were not so apparent to him and he did not consider an effort to escape. After the death of Hugh Hall and prior to the date of the sale he did contemplate escape on one or two occasions.

In one instance he and another slave had planned an attempt to escape, but the other Negro took two more slaves into the plan and Samuel Hall knowing them to be drinking boys refused to go with them. They got up into Illinois, got into a saloon and then into trouble and were finally turned back to their owners.

One of the most ingenious plans suggested to Samuel for his escape was one proposed by a white man named Lundee. Lundee suggested to Samuel Hall that they run away together and he, Lundee, would sell Hall and secure the necessary money to carry them on up through the northern states into Canada. After Lundee had sold Mr. Hall, Mr. Hall was to run away again and join Lundee and then they would go on.

This plan sounded all right to Mr. Hall, providing he could be sure that Lundee would be honest with him. But, since the scheme contemplated a dishonest act on the part of Lundee right to start with, in selling property that didn't belong to him, Mr. Hall questioned the good faith of the man making the proposition. He refused to go into that plan.

Samuel Hall, 47 Years a Slave

A white girl of considerable property offered to take Sam north as her slave and free him in Canada, if he would run away, but there was a terrible danger in such an attempt and it meant more than danger to the girl who proposed the plan and Samuel Hall refused to avail himself of that chance which he felt was a chance in the strictest sense of the word. And so it was that he was taken to the block and sold.

WILLIAM WALLACE'S SLAVE.

THE PURCHASER of Samuel Hall was a man by the name of William Wallace. He was what was known at that time as a "pillar" in the Presbyterian church in his home community which was on the Tennessee-Mississippi border line nine hundred miles from where Samuel Hall had been sold. The trip was made by wagon all that distance and Mr. Hall was in this man's service for about ten years.

The story of his experience with this "saintly" character will be told later in Mr. Hall's own words. It was during his service for this man that he was married a second time and this time he was again wedded to the woman slave of a neighbor and he had five children in slavery by this wife. That wife and their five children were brought north by Mr. Hall at the close of the great war which freed the slaves.

At the very beginning of the war, at the time of the John Brown raid, the

Negroes in the community in which Mr. Hall was living became somewhat excited over the situation and it was suspicioned by the whites that they planned to organize an uprising and had chosen Mr. Hall as their captain. During that time of excitement Mr. Hall did not know what moment he might be led out by the whites and hanged to a tree until he was dead. But that all passed over and later he was gathered in with many other reluctant slaves to help do the hard work for the soldiers in the Southern army.

His faithful service in that way tended to make the soldiers feel that they had in him a good rebel. He served in the rebel army, taking care of horses most of the time for about two years. While he was in appearance a good rebel he was at heart the opposite. He had a pretty good understanding of the situation and was content to bide his time. Meanwhile he never lost an opportunity to favor the union army in a surreptitious way and was on several different occasions in the union lines and in conference with union officers. He knew better, however, than to run away permanently from the south and from his master for still, by all legal rights he was the property of William Wallace; therefore he remained nominally a slave.

    The union army gradually crowded down into Tennessee so threateningly that the Southerners began to fear the loss of their slaves. Samuel Hall was put in with a bunch of other valuable Negroes and started south as a refugee. Mr. Hall started, not entirely aware of the significance of the move, but after he had traveled a day he came to himself and getting up the next morning hitched up his team of mules and when the man in charge of the refugees asked him what he was doing he said he was getting ready to go back home.

    He said: "I ain't going another damned step south."

    He went back home and immediately William Wallace got up a big party for Sam. All the colored folks of the community were invited in to make merry at the celebration in honor of Mr. Wallace's returned foreman. At this party Samuel Hall was the gayest of the gay. No one would have thought, to see him, that he had a single other thought than thoughts of gratitude toward his dear master. He danced and he sang and he ate as happily as one would who was without a care and the next morning he was gone. The emancipation proclamation had been issued just two days before and Sam knew now that he was permanently safe with the union army and he went to it.

A CHANCE FOR REVENGE.

IT WAS but a few days after he joined the union army that Samuel Hall had an opportunity for revenge over his old master that few men would have failed to take advantage of. He feared that his family might be taken south as refugees, since they were still in slavery, and he secured a band of union soldiers and went to his old master's plantation to get his family. In the flush of his new liberty he said things to his old master which he admits now he should not have said.

He showed William Wallace the scar on his neck where Wallace had almost succeeded in making a fatal cut in Sam's throat and he delivered himself of a few thoughts that were not calculated to ease Wallace's peace of mind. Union soldiers standing by told Sam to beat the man's brains out.

Mrs. Wallace in a frenzy of terror begged for mercy for her husband and she with the restraining influence of Sam prevailed upon the bunch of union soldiers not to harm Wallace personally. They gave Sam complete charge of the situation, however, so that his revenge at that time was of an undreamed of spectacular character. He required no more of his old master, however, than that that ex-master should hitch up his mules, load up his wagon with hams and bacon and include in the load Sam's wife and five children and haul them all over into the union lines.

In a few days Mr. Hall with his family and many other Negroes got on board a boat and moved northward, forever away from the unhappy south. Mr. Hall says that as the boat pulled out into the river the colored people sang the most beautiful song that he has ever heard. His old master stood by the side of the river tearfully watching the disappearance of his $1,125.00 and Sam waved his old hat in farewell to that man who was never more to issue orders to him. Mr. Wallace had found out that Sam was just what they had told him in

North Carolina, "a damned good nigger, but he knowed too much." Wallace had come down to the river to beg Sam to come back onto his plantation. He was ready to make any kind of terms with him but Sam wouldn't listen to them. He was bound to get clear away from the scene of the most unhappy days of his life. He was forty-seven years of age before he came into his own rights as a man and after serving the full term of his enlistment in the union army he brought his family on up into Washington county, Iowa, which has been his home ever since. The following is Mr. Hall's own story as written in his own words, telling additional incidents in his own life.

SAMUEL HALL'S STORY.

EARLIEST RECOLLECTIONS.

"I WAS born May 7th, 1818, in Iredell County, N. C., of slave parents, whose forefathers were full-blooded Africans. My father could well remember when he was shipped over. He was born in Liberia and he and his mother were kidnaped when he was 15 years of age and they were brought over to this country and sold as slaves. The mother never would work, but pined away and died. She never learned the American language. My father had two brothers who were never brought over.

When I was a little boy, one of the first things that I can remember was that my uncle had a fish trap and I went with him down to his fish trap and when we got in sight of his fish trap a man by the name of Will Hall had taken one fish out and we were so close to him that he didn't have time to get away with the fish so he jumped in the creek and swam across and as we came back--it, was in the spring of the year and the old geese had goslings and in those days we boys wore nothing but shirts and I was behind my uncle watching him when the old gander took offense at my light clothing and decided to whip me and succeeded in so far that my uncle had to take him off me.

The next thing I can remember was when my youngest brother walked. My brother stuck a butcher knife in the floor and told him to walk and he walked to it and he was so tickled to see him walk that he grabbed him and went to sit down on the tub where my mother was washing and in they both went. That happened just ninty years ago March, 1911.

A little later I can remember that the Negro where I was raised had to have so many days out of each week to be taught. When I got up so I could learn the law was changed so that my people could have no schooling. But the man that raised me being opposed to the law decided that his Negroes should read and he gave us a chance to learn and brother Peter was the only one that took the chance for learning. But I was taken to Sabbath school and taught in respect to the Bible ever since I was a small boy.

Every Sabbath we had a long bench set in the yard and that was where we had our Sabbath school at home, but the main Sabbath school was held in the Academy where my master taught; but in a short time that was shut off, then there was no more Sabbath school for my people. Then the law was passed in a short time that whoever was caught teaching the Negro they would have to pay a big fine.

THE NEGRO KEPT IN DARKNESS

This brings me up to about the time when I began to learn to read. I had an old elementary speller and my master and his children taught me how to spell but I did not take on enough learning and my master would say to me: "old fellow you will rue it," which I have. Later my eyes were opened and I could see the great mistake I had made, for from the day they began to shut off the learning from the Negro they began to bind them fighter. If the Negro ever learned to write and it was made known the law was that he or she must suffer the loss of a finger to keep him from writing.

It leads me here to impress on the people that everything possible has been done to keep the Negro in darkness and yet, with all the oppression that was put upon him, to keep the Negro in darkness, when Christmas came and New Years, although some would be sold and going with their blankets and bundles on their backs and heads, they were far more happy than their oppressors and yet the people of the north would come among my people and speak about them being so happy, but for all that they didn't realize what the burdens of the race were.

    Yes, they were happy during the holidays up to New Years but at that time many of them would be changing homes and their burdens would be very heavy. And, oh, such heavy tasks as they would be put to! So heavy that some of them could not endure them, no more than a horse with more than he can pull and becomes balky.

    The men who had wives would go to see them twice a week, Wednesday and Saturday, and they might stay to see them over Sabbath, some of them. Wherever that man had a wife, the children of said wife belonged to the wife's master and the father of the children had no control over his children and the children were raised to tell their master whatever was talked about during this visit.

And in those days the southern country was patrolled by what they called patrollers. Those men would come into our place of enjoyment and drive and whip the husbands away from their wives and use those same women for their own pleasure. Then how could our women live virtuous lives with such treatment as they had to endure. I have known these slave holders to take and sell husband and wife away from each other just for spite when they would attempt to stand up for their virtue.

MY FIRST MARRIAGE.

This brings me to the time of my own marriage. I was married to my first wife May 6th, 1844, by Squire Dunlap, of North Carolina. The license then was a permit from my master and a permit from her master. If that was agreeable, that was all that was necessary. They gave me a big wedding at her master's home. He respected me and wanted me in his family, but would not buy me when I was sold for the reason that I had been raised to know that I was a man and they always called me a "free nigger."

I lived with this wife not quite twelve years. Then my master died and his Negroes were sold because our mistress was afraid to keep us so that sale was on for all of us. I was the first one put on the block and was bid off the block for $1,125.00. I was sold to a man by the name of William Wallace who lived on the line of Mississippi and Tennessee. I was sold away from my wife and children and was taken nine hundred miles away from them and never saw any of them anymore, excepting two of the children that I sent and brought north twelve years after I came here.

TAKEN TO TENNESSEE.

After I was sold I was taken to Fayette county, Tennessee, and lived there ten years. With this I began to see the awful curse of slavery. My master said when he bought me that he was going to take me down to Tennessee and "break me." I had never been broken.

He took me and I lived with him three years before I ever attempted to get out among the young people, then trouble began. I went to him and asked him one Saturday evening for a pass, and he said with an oath that he did not buy me to run around among the girls, I was to wait on him.

"Now," said I, "you sell me, for we will never get along, for you can kill me but you can't whip me."

He said, "I'll sell you to the devil."

I said: "You can sell me to the devil, or any other place, but you can't whip me. I'll never ask you for a pass again, but when I have my work done I am going!"

I went and put on my Sunday clothes and went away and after I had gone he wrote a pass and said I was "too big feelin' " to wait and from that time on he had it made up in his mind to whip me. I had been foreman on his plantation all the time from the time he bought me, but on Wednesday night I was away and on Thursday morning he called me up and asked me where I had been and I told him and he swore by an oath that he was going to have something done and I said:

"You sell me, or kill me."

And he said: "I'll sell you to the devil."

And I said: "I don't care who in the devil you sell me to."

WALLACE TRIES TO "TAKE ME."

My master changed my work and when he changed my work I put the boys to ploughing and I went up after the tools to start them to work. When I came back with the tools he was waiting on the fence and he said to me: "I am going to take you down this morning."

I said: "I guess not!"

There were three colored boys there and he thought he and the three boys would take me. I dropped my tools and took up a hoe and said:

"Any man that comes to me, I'll kill him, I don't care who it is."

Then he picked up a piece of rail and threw it at me and ran. It hit me and hurt me but I didn't let on. The coward went home and got the gun and came back and I was sitting on the fence.

He said: "Now by G-- I guess you'll get down.

I said to him: "If you shoot that gun off shoot to kill me, for if you shoot to scare me I'll kill you sure."

Then he wheeled around and ran and directly he came back with two other men that were called "nigger breakers." I was still sitting on the fence but was prepared for a fight. I had got me a good club and was sitting on the fence in such a way that I could get over which ever way they came.

And so, here they came, himself with the two "nigger breakers" and a doctor and he had a loaded whip, the end of it being filled with lead about ten inches long. He aimed at me with the whip and the end flew out and hit one of the men on the arm and crippled him. I was on the one side of the fence and they on the other and I defied them to come over but they were afraid. They worked for about two hours begging me to just let them tie me, but I wouldn't do it. I told them that they could kill me right then and there but they shouldn't tie me.

After while a friend of mine[, Billy] Tomblin, a white man, came up and asked Wallace, my master, what the trouble was and Wallace said:

"This nigger has got the 'big' in him and I want to take it out."

Then Billy Tomblin said: "Wallace you have got the best nigger in the country and he don't need no whippin'.".

Then Wallace got mad and they both got mad and Tomblin swore right then and there that they should not whip me. After they had fussed a while my master wanted me to go back to work but I had it in my head that he must sell me, but he said that if I would go back to work it would be settled and I could go on as I had before. So Billy Tomblin persuaded me to go back to work and it would be all right so I agreed if they were sure it was settled.

TRIES TO CUT MY THROAT.

I went back to work and still my master had that old grudge against me that he would break me and I knew it. In just a year from that time he had set his mind to take me again. I had been away all day on the Sabbath and he didn't say a thing to me about it, but on Monday he went and got two of what they called "bully men" and they were going to take me. On Tuesday when I came to my dinner he and two other men were sitting on the porch and I passed by them and looked at them and they looked at me but I went on around to the kitchen for my dinner. My mistress did not call her men in to dinner until I passed by going to my dinner, then she came to the kitchen window and said:

"Sam, they are going to take you, and I wish you were dead."

I said right there and then: "I'll soon be dead, for they never will take me."

She said: "It will be a terrible thing."

I sat down and ate my dinner and then stayed in and took my smoke as usual. We always had an hour and a half at noon. Then I got up and went to the barn. In the meantime one of the men had gone out and got behind the barn.

In those days the barns were made with legs. Then my master and the other fellow came following me to the barn and when I went into the barn the one that was behind the barn came around and the two of them were coming in the door and one of them said:

"Sam, I guess we'll have to take you down."

But there were entries made in the barn and bars to keep the horses from backing into the entries. I took one bar down and dropped it and carried the other one with me up to the head of the horses very unconcerned. When they said they would have to take me, I said: "I guess not," and I made for them and ran them out of the barn and started to go out of the barn myself. My master was standing at the side of the door with a knife in his hand and I did not see him and he tried to cut my throat. He succeeded so far that he just missed the jugular vein, striking me in the jaw with the knife. Then he ran and me after them, the blood flying from my face and neck.

    I chased them out of the barn yard and then for forty-eight hours no one could come near me, not even my wife who wanted to wrap up my neck. I was crazy mad and did not care if I died. I just let the cut in my neck and jaw go.

    When I came to my senses the "nigger breakers" had gone and my master came to me and apologized, saying that he was wrong and begging me to go back to work, but I would not go to work for a week or more and then I was persuaded to by friends and finally did and never had any more trouble with him as long as I stayed. After that he was offered $1,900.00 for me and he would not take it. That was in the spring of 1858.

MY SECOND MARRIAGE.

I was married to my second wife in September, 1857, and we lived together fifty years and six months. To us nine children were born, three dead and six living. My wife and my master's wife were full cousins. After this trouble with my master I had made my mind to run off and go to Canada, I and another man by the name of Mart Burnette, but he took in two other fellows and when he did that I was afraid because I knew that they drank and I was afraid to risk them. So they started and went off and went up into Illinois and went into a saloon and when they went into the saloon they got into trouble and were asked for their pass and they had none. Then they were taken to St. Louis and put in jail and lay there for three months and were advertised for sale, and their masters went up and got them and brought them back and put them in old Ed Forrest's trader yard and their masters would go in and whip them three times a day.

How cruel! They were kept there two weeks, or until they found some one to buy them, and one of them was whipped nearly to death. Mart Burnette in about three months after he was sold down below Vicksburg came back after me to go with him to Canada. I was away and he couldn't see me, but if I had been home I should have gone. I never saw him any more for he got to Canada and wrote back to his master and said: "I am in Canada, now you come and get me."

Old Ed Forrest was the General Forrest who was in the southern army. He kept a slave trader yard in Memphis and I knew him well. I saw him often when I was in Memphis for my master. He would buy up slaves and keep them in this yard and sell them like people sell hogs today. He did a big business and was known all over the south. His trader yard was always filled full of slaves for sale or trade, and the danger of the freeing of the slaves made old Ed fear that his business was going to be knocked out. That was the reason he fought so hard for the south. He didn't want his "nigger pen" put out of business.

CRUELTIES OF SLAVERY.

I knew an old man who was whipped to death by his master. I saw the old man after he was whipped so hard. The master took a "nigger" whip and doubled it and whipped the old man until there were splits in his side where the whip doubled over. The old man lived several days after the whipping and one night I was out fishing and while I was sitting on the bank in the dark fishing I heard a voice praying and it was the old man. He had crawled out into the brush and he was praying for his master, that the master might be brought to see the light. God says "Blessed are the merciful, for they shall inherit the earth." My people have always been merciful. God will keep his promise in his own good-time; in his own good way.

I have seen slave mothers fall over in a dead faint when their children were sold away from them. The mothers would have to hand down their children and when they fell over in a faint men would pick the poor women up and carry them away just as if they were dogs. Those mothers loved their little children just the same as white mothers love their little babies and some of them were never happy again and some went insane as did my old mother when her children were sold away from her.

My first wife's sister was killed by her master. He struck her over the head with a loaded cane. We did not know that for some time after the girl's death for slaves feared to tell such things for fear they would be killed for telling.

My boy, Frank, was taken by William Wallace down into the brush and whipped and Wallace told Frank that if he told me he would kill him. Wallace knew me so well that he feared to let me know that he had whipped one of my boys. Frank never told me about it until after we were up north, clear away from any danger from Wallace.

THE LITTLE CHILDREN.

Now I want to speak about how the little children were treated. I have seen where these "nigger" traders would go and buy children from eight years down to babies. To feed them they would have a pan about ten or fifteen feet long and put a row of these children on each side of it and they would make soup of vegetables and these children would just eat and slap and fight like pigs over swill. They were cared for by an old woman whose charge it was to look after them like we do hogs. They were raised to do just like what you would tell a dog to do. When they would come to ten or eleven years old they would be put on the block and sold.

The poor mothers had to hand their children down to those "nigger" traders" just the same as you would sell a calf away from a cow. No matter how her heart would ache she would have to see her little child go, and yet one-third of said children would probably have white fathers and the very one that was patrolled out to keep the negro in his place would often be the father to some of these children.

Now I want to know what the reader thinks of this inhuman treatment toward my people when your people went into the wilds of Africa and brought the Negroes here among enlightened people and placed him here as a slave and kept him in bondage nigh unto three centuries; used them like dogs, yes even placed them lower than a dog, used him to his own advantage and yet they want the Negro problem solved. Suppose they had begun solving this years sooner and remembered that he was flesh and blood the same as you and others of different nationalities that they are sending the light to by missionaries. Suppose they had begun working on us to enlighten us instead of kicking us lower and lower. The problem would have been solved years ago, yes years ago.

Tell me what the Negro has done to make him a slave. Sure, he has his bad with his good ones, so have the white people, but there has never been anything done that was right but what he stood by it as a man. Show me if you please what reproach the Negro has ever brought on this nation. No sir, he has been loyal to his nation. God said "blessed are the peace makers" and this the loyal Negro believes in.

  But, slavery has been God's doing. God was in it. It was a blessing to the black man and a curse to the white man. It brought my people from savagery and gave us the enlightenment of the American people. There are black men in Africa now who went over from here who are doing ten times more good than a white man can for the people of Africa know they are their own people. There was lots of suffering for the black people in slavery but it had its purpose. The Children of Israel were in slavery, too. That was God's plan. Joseph was sold up into Egypt; we were stolen and brought over into America. God was in all of it.

Samuel Hall, 47 Years a Slave

I thank you for reading my story and may God bless you as he has blessed me with long life and may your latter days be as happy as mine have been..

SAMUEL HALL.

SAMUEL HALL'S LATER LIFE.

THAT THEN is Samuel Hall's story as written by himself. He was rather meagre in his details, therefore this writer added to the story the opening and more detailed outline of his career. However, his life in all of its strange vicissitudes offers abundant room for a long, long story. But this work was for the purpose only of putting in black and white, for Mr. Hall's own satisfaction, a few of the incidents of his long life, and also to express to the people of Washington county, Iowa, Mr. Hall's appreciation of the good treatment that he and his family has always received from them.

The next forty-seven years of Mr. Hall's life can be told in even fewer words. He was forty-seven years of age at the time that he was freed from slavery and at the time of this writing he has enjoyed just about forty-seven years more of free life. They have been beautiful years to him, too. He has enjoyed them all and he expects to go right on enjoying this life and finally quietly blend it into that grander and better life about which he has read and thought now for over ninety years.

As a little black youngster, barely able to toddle about, his first master "Alex Hall" used to gather the slaves about him Sunday afternoons in the yard of his home and teach them about God and Heaven and there it was that Samuel Hall learned about God and became a thorough convert to the principles that are the essence of real Christianity.

In some of the more stirring experiences of his life he had his trials, his temptations, and made his mistakes, as all others have done. But those little lessons that he learned in his master's Sunday school when he was a small boy kept him steadfast in the Christian faith and undoubtedly were the means of preserving his life through the trying years of his later slave life.

Immediately after the close of the civil war Samuel Hall, his wife and his five children came to Washington, Iowa. Mr. Hall had planned to go to Wisconsin, but while in Memphis serving out the time of his enlistment with the union army he fell in with Major James Hope and Captain Allen and he liked them and concluded to go where they went. They came back to Washington and here Mr. Hall came as an entire stranger, a perfectly black man, with a black wife and five coal black children. It was like coming into a new world to them, but the manner of Mr. Hall's rearing had in a way prepared him for the change in his conditions and he soon adapted himself to the ways of the north.

HIS LIFE IN WASHINGTON.

MR. HALL moved his family into a little house up in the east end of Washington and there they lived for three days. In the meantime, he had been looking for work. John Hale saw him, liked his appearance and approached him to ask him what kind of work he wanted to do. Sam told him that he wanted any kind of work, so Mr. Hale hired him to farm for him. He farmed for John Hale for four years, managing the farm entirely and retired from that work only to go into farming for himself.

At the very beginning of his work in the north he had some little humiliations to endure, but they were as nothing to what he had had to endure as a slave so they seemed as comparatively nothing to him. They hurt his pride a little, but in doing that they spurred him to greater honorable effort in order that he might show the white men that there were some good Negroes.

One citizen of Washington prominent in that day wondered why John Hale was "taking a lot of damned 'niggers' out to his place to steal everything he had." Mr. Hall heard of the remark and long after, when he had "proved himself" and after he had become intimately acquainted with that "prominent citizen" he recalled the saying to the mind of the citizen and had the satisfaction of hearing the old gentleman admit that he had been fooled in Sam Hall and his family.

Shortly after moving out onto the Hale farm the matter of schooling for his children came up. There was objection in the district on the part of some of the families to permitting the Negroes to go to school with their children. One farmer said that if Hall's children were going to be permitted to go to school in that district his children should stay at home. S. P. Kiefer, still a resident of this community was one of the directors and he said that Hall's children "were going to school in that district and the other man could keep his children at home if he wanted to." That didn't happen, however. The disgruntled farmer sent his children to school just the same and inside of three weeks they were the most friendly of all the children in the school toward Mr. Hall's children.

At the close of his service with John Hale, Mr. Hall bought a little farm of Dr. McClelland west of town. That he farmed for a while and then he sold it and planned to go to Kansas. Before getting started west, however, he changed his mind and bought teams and again went to farming for himself. He rented from Dr. McClelland for two years; from Michael Hayes for five years; from Alex Houck for three years, and then he came into Washington where he has since lived. He accumulated enough property to see him safely through his old age and he saw all his children started well in life so far as education could start them.

He always felt that education was the one thing that was needed to bring his people up. The right kind of education he says will solve the Negro problem. It must be an education that teaches industry and frugality. If the Negro will go his own way, work, do his work well, be honest and treat all men right, Mr. Hall insists that he will be respected and will not be subjected to the humiliations and reproaches that are heaped upon the less worthy.

He knows there is a prejudice against the Negro that is deep seated and generally very unjust. It is a prejudice that is to a certain extent based upon that often illustrated principle which is shown in one's dislike for one whom he has injured. The south injured the Negro, took unfair advantage of him and now in his life of so-called freedom the people of the south, pricked by an uneasy conscience, still, in many instances, strive to justify themselves and in so doing evidence their hatred of the Negro as a free man in this country.

Samuel Hall is an interesting old colored man. Mental and physical strength have been happily blended into his make-up. He is optimistic in temperament; well satisfied to take the events of the day as they come, having faith in the outcome and believing that all things are for the best to them that "love the Lord."

He has always been highly respected by those who knew him and those who have known him intimately know that he is made of the kind of stuff that heroes are built from. In authorizing the publication of this short story of his life he did it, not because he felt that his life was entitled to any greater publicity than the lives of thousands of others, but because he wanted to express in some public way the great sense of gratitude which he feels toward the people of the community in which he has lived his free life. He says:

"I want the people of Washington and Washington county to know that I have always tried to live like a man among them and to be in my conduct as nearly like them as I could. I didn't want them to see anything different about me excepting my skin, and I have always claimed that if a man is as black as coal, but behaves himself and tends to his own business and don't shove himself in where he ain't wanted, he'll get along all right and will be wanted more and more places as he grows older. You tell the people of Washington county that they've always been good to me and my family and we all thank them for it. Iowa is the best state in the union toward the Negro and Iowa has always tried to help me and my people."

Samuel Hall, 47 Years a Slave

Samuel Hall, 47 Years a Slave

www.ingramcontent.com/pod-product-compliance
Lightning Source LLC
LaVergne TN
LVHW041345080426
835512LV00006B/624